Praise for *It's Time to Brag! Business Edition*

It's Time to Brag! is a necessary book. Too many of us suppress our genius because we think that sharing our skills and our accomplishments is too showy, too braggy. And while it's great when others credential our expertise with a testimonial or recommendation, we can't control how or when they do it. We can only control our words. So step up and learn how to brag! While it might not come naturally to many people, bragging is a skill we must learn as business professionals.

Was I comfortable claiming the name "LinkedIn expert"? Hell no! But by working with Jeannette and claiming my own power and expertise, I grabbed the moniker and not only has it proven to be true, it's positioned me as one of the leading social media experts in the world. So read the book, already!

—Viveka von Rosen, Founder of Linked into Business;
Author of *LinkedIn Marketing: An Hour a Day*, *LinkedIn Security: Who's Watching You*, and *LinkedIn: 101 Ways to Rock Your Personal Brand*; and Top 50 Forbes Social Media Influencer for four years

It's Time to Brag! Business Edition *has not only helped me sell myself in networking meetings, it has also helped me grow our employee benefits business. Six months after reading Jeannette's book, I've been able to add 15 new insurance product offerings to our existing client base of 80 customers, which has increased our revenue by 25 percent. A clear, professional brag statement can be a powerful tool to bring credibility and show expertise in your line of work.*

—Paul Rizzo, Employee Benefits Broker/Consultant,
Innovative Benefit Solutions, LLC

Too often, we fail to take time and look at our many achievements. We tell ourselves they don't matter. Having built an award-winning business for the past 16 years, from $0 and now selling it for just *under $.5M, I know that bragging is very important. It's important in any business venture to build credibility immediately in a highly competitive industry, and to keep it. Being confident and learning to brag about your accomplishments when meeting with clients is necessary to grow your business. The more confident you are, the more your clients will want to work with you.*

—Suzan Simmons, Partner, Fourest, LLC

Jeannette's book has encouraged us to identify and brag about measures of results with our clients. Telling our stats surely inspires people—we have been married for 46 years, in business for 40 years, and have touched tens of thousands of lives. Ms. Seibly artfully conveys simple ways to attract more business based on past and current successes!

—Ruth Sharon, M.S., Licensed Professional Counselor, and Jim Sharon, Ed.D., Licensed Psychologist; Coaches, Seminar Leaders, and Authors of four books, most recently *Secrets of a Soulful Marriage* (SkyLight Paths, 2014); voted Best Relationship Coaches in 2015 and 2016; Founders of Energy for Life

Before, I believed in the paradigm "I have to do more, I'm not there yet," so I was unreasonable in pushing my team for more. After I wrote down my Knowledge, Talents, and Achievements, I could see how much I had accomplished. My whole view about myself changed. After this breakthrough, I started to see my team from a new angle and I started to appreciate their achievements. As a result, I learned to relax while still focusing on the intended results. For example, since reading the Brag book, I've put in place one new system to reduce employee turnover by 10 percent and added a new coaching program that enables our management team to enjoy our many raving fans.

—Cristina Elena Nistor, Director of Operations, TESTCo Mexico

Jeannette has a wonderful way of getting people to brag about themselves. As a contributor to my Wealthy Women Empowering Wealthy Women leads group, she helped the women create confidence in sharing their success with others. For example, I am blessed by doubling my income for five years in a row. As a result of my efforts, I have moved into the top 3 percent of Realtors with Coldwell Banker nationwide. Whether you are new in your business or seasoned, Jeannette's book will give you a fresh idea on how to share your success. Keep playing BIG!

—Faith Young, Author of *What Would Faith DO?*
and Top Realtor with Coldwell Banker

Not long ago, I evidently stunned a friend to disbelief and incredulity by revealing that I'd attended an internationally renowned global business school where I earned my MBA. That's when I knew I needed a book like this more than I realized. Jeannette Seibly's newest work offers great insight about how to get out of our own way, many exercises and examples to build upon, and will have you out using effective new communication skills almost immediately. What I especially see has made a difference for me is how Jeannette helped me reframe the distaste I felt about bragging into an expression of my results, leveraging the inner joy and enthusiasm for the things I've accomplished.

—Jennifer Scholfield, Consultant

Before you attend another networking event, read Jeannette's book. It's Time to Brag! is extremely readable, provocative, yet practical. By using Jeannette's five-step process, I was able to differentiate myself at networking events and conferences. I saw a 20 percent jump in my initial meeting sets! I highly recommend it for any individual or organization that is looking to attain the next level of success.

—Jim Molloy, Financial Advisor

In It's Time to Brag!, *author Jeannette Seibly masterfully walks the reader through how to organize their successes in clear and concise terms, enabling them to confidently brag about their accomplishments. As a result, people pay attention to your message. Bottom line—it works. Over the last 12 months I have seen a 32 percent increase in one-on-one meetings from utilizing this bragging process.*

—Bill Saltz, Senior Director, Associate, LegalShield;
www.BillSaltz.com

Being in the material handling and packaging industry for 40 years, one might consider me to be an expert in my field. What I learned from Jeannette's book was that often times I do not brag enough or correctly. In addition to using this great tool, I find that one-on-one sessions with a coach on a regular basis keep me on point and accountable.

—John P. Rizzo, Material Handling Manager, Pak West

Jeannette Seibly's book It's Time to Brag! *provided me with straightforward, no-nonsense advice about how to effectively share my unique story with prospective clients, and to pack an early and powerful message into the first stage of a conversation. Her book and her seminars use questions that probe deeply, and they offered me the opportunity to get to the heart of what sets my business apart and makes my skill set unique. Seibly forced me to think about, quantify, and communicate the impact I've had on the clients and the community I serve. Her probing and coaching made me stop and reflect on my own story. With the help of Seibly's fine-tuning, quantifying and verbalizing my accomplishments has been a confidence builder that opens naturally into a dialog about how I can help my clients.*

—Jeanette Meyer, Principal, Meyer and Associates

Jeannette Seibly's book gives the business entrepreneur permission to brag. Using her methods, I joined a pre-launch network marketing company and within weeks, my team was one of the fastest growing teams company-wide, with 15 promotions in a seven-week window. Not only were we recognized by top leadership, but they wanted to know what we were doing. We were bragging. People want to be a part of a winning team! I taught my team to brag and our results became explosive.

I also use Jeannette's method in both my traditional and virtual assistant businesses, where my team of five serves over 100 businesses with a growing six figures in annual sales.

—Michele Reynolds, Sapphire Ambassador, Wakaya Perfection, Founder and CEO, Success Troops LLC Virtual Assistant Business

A Note from Jeannette

Thank you to those who wrote testimonials for this book. It takes courage to brag, and even more courage to put those achievements in writing. Remember to get your brag on! Your career and life successes, and your future financial rewards, will thank you!

It's Time To
BRAG!

Business Edition

Five Amazing Steps
To Sell Yourself

Jeannette L. Seibly

It's Time to Brag! Business Edition
Five Amazing Steps To Sell Yourself
©2017 Jeannette L. Seibly

ISBN: 978-0-9847415-3-3 (eBook)
ISBN: 978-0-9847415-4-0 (Print)

Library of Congress Control Number: 2016952605

Editor: Faith Marcovecchio, Faith Marcovecchio Editorial

Design: Nick Zelinger, NZ Graphics

BizSavvy Books
P.O. Box 631473
Highlands Ranch, CO 80163-1473

Also by Jeannette Seibly:

Hire Amazing Employees, Second Edition
It's Time to Brag!
It's Time to Brag! Career Edition

CONTENTS

*"If you can't sell yourself,
you can't sell your product or services!"*
– Jeannette L. Seibly

INTRODUCTION

You have less than 4.3 minutes to create credibility at the beginning of any presentation.

You have less than 15 seconds to attract interest when networking.

It's up to you to create a remarkable and lasting impression.

Your success requires you to talk with others in a business-savvy manner!

All of us are taught at a very early age that bragging is wrong. It simply is not a nice thing to do. It's rude and shows poor manners. The fear is we will be thought of as braggarts. Or worse, we fear being laughed at or ridiculed for our hubris.

We learned during our years growing up that we must be humble about our accomplishments … often to our own detriment. What happens when we fail to share our accomplishments with others?

- We lose recognition and clients when we don't step up to share our successes—people are not mind readers.
- We fail to obtain awards for government contracts when we underrepresent our past achievements.
- We get bypassed for promotions or prized job assignments when others—in particular our bosses—are unclear about our accomplishments.

- We are unable to clearly establish our credentials in sales presentations.
- We are unaware of how to acquire invaluable "insider" information when networking.

This is the era of relationships. Social media connections have moved us into being connected with others, and usually we stay in touch with them personally and professionally to build on those relationships. People like to work with winners. So in order to convey that you are a winner, it is important for you to effectively share your achievements in a business-savvy manner and encourage others to connect with you.

This means putting down the phone! Most business professionals today prefer connecting with others via texts, emails, and other messaging methods. The problem is, those communication methods are not highly proficient in uncovering new opportunities and important nuances, and they can often lead to misunderstandings. Unfortunately, the wrong word or phrase can cause a disconnection before you've had a chance to get to know another person. Make it a habit to meet others face to face, including via Skype, FaceTime, and other conferencing methods. That way, when you follow up using electronic methods, there is less chance for miscommunication. (See *Chapter 9: Networking Works* for further details.)

A manager and her team were seated at a company function when her boss was called to the front of the room. The president of this multimillion-dollar marketing company acknowledged the boss for the work the manager and her team had accomplished. Imagine their surprise when the boss didn't mention them!

> *Later, one on one and in private, the manager asked her boss, "Why didn't you acknowledge me and the team?" His only response was, "Someday you will learn how to brag!"*

Our unwillingness to be in the spotlight and track our success metrics stops us from achieving our professional goals. This reluctance stays with us even as we are overlooked for promotions, sales contracts, key job assignments, or industry recognition.

What's missing? Not sharing our achievements in a business-savvy manner.

To develop a stronger self-image as a confident business professional, some falsely believe you simply need to "feel it." However, confidence alone does not necessarily help you speak in a businesslike manner or speak up so you are heard. When you are able to brag so others readily understand and value your results, your confidence and competence naturally speak volumes. Then others no longer dismiss your experiences and credentials or fail to listen to how you can make a positive difference in the business environment.

There is a missing link!

***

A key component to bragging effectively is to be authentic and clear. Too often when people talk with networking contacts (e.g., people we meet and connect with at a formal meeting, conference meet-and-greet, trade or meet-up event, etc.) or submit contract bids, they attempt to sound like others. If you are not able to distinguish yourself from everybody else with the clarity of your achievements, or if you sound too creative and people can't identify with what you're saying, you've lost out on current and future opportunities with them, and access to their contacts.

Many people find it difficult to set up and conduct networking meetings because they have not differentiated themselves in a way that makes others wish to talk with them. They forget people want to meet and know winners.

Another component to bragging well is being prepared. Some falsely believe they can wing it in a presentation or a networking meeting. They don't honor their contacts by preparing for the meetings, and lack the know-how to obtain insider information. (Note: This also requires putting down the phone and not texting while others are talking! You will miss important opportunities!)

Networking is marketing, conducting further research, educating yourself about different possibilities, and sharing information with confidence. It's letting others know of your understanding of an industry, profession, or company while obtaining additional insider information. **Sales calls are for selling**. You can't effectively network and make a sales call at the same time … this is one of the biggest mistakes made in networking meetings.

(Note: This book is designed to help business owners, executives, consultants, marketing/sales reps, and everyone else do a better job of selling themselves. It does not replace, nor is it intended to replace, a qualified sales system, but will simply enhance the process for better results.)

I attended a networking meeting and met a woman who had read the first edition of this book. She shared with me two

> statements, the one she used to use at networking meetings and her revised "brag" statement.
>
> Original statement: *My company provides residential roofing.*
>
> Brag statement: *I am a sales rep for a 34-year-old roofing company that has replaced over 35,000 roofs!*
>
> I was so impressed by the difference that when I met a realtor, I brought her over to meet the roofing company sales rep. The realtor was so impressed by the "brag" statement that she quickly provided two hot referrals!
>
> She said to me, "I've had those referrals for a couple of days and didn't know who to give them to."
>
> I've seen this happen countless times. People are so impressed by effective bragging that they immediately come up with referrals.

It's time to get over your shyness or fear. It's time to learn how to make a positive and lasting impression. In order for you to win the sales presentation, win the contract, or receive the promotion or business recognition, you need to:

- Share your accomplishments in a business-savvy manner
- Establish immediate credibility and interest
- Sell yourself first in a sales meeting
- Provide clarity and differentiation in contract bids, award nominations, and sales proposals
- Develop a better understanding of a company's or industry's issues as a result of networking meetings *before* a sales call
- Be heard and be seen in a business-savvy way that compels others to take positive notice!

Act Like a Cat

**"You can't sell yourself if you are unable to speak about your results in a businesslike manner."
—Jeannette Seibly**

The key purpose of this book is to help you understand how to:

- Establish credibility immediately and in a professional manner
- Garner insider information faster in networking meetings
- Set up and manage introductions for effective client meetings
- Impress judges with your value and accomplishments when reading your nomination for a business award
- Differentiate yourself in sales proposals, contract bids, websites, brochures, and marketing materials
- And most of all, be seen as confident and competent

Why are these important? *Because you are an amazing person with amazing accomplishments! (You may wish to reread that statement several times and let it sink in!)* Sharing your successes so that others hear you and listen to you makes all the difference.

© Jeannette L. Seibly, 2013

This picture is to remind you how you look when you attempt to look like everyone else, sound like everyone else, or plagiarize others' accomplishments.

Too often we pretend we are raccoons when in fact we're cats. Everyone knows we're cats. The raccoons know we're not like them. The raccoons expect us to act like a cat when we are interacting with them. Obviously, as a cat you can never be a raccoon. Attempting to be something you are not is unimpressive, even when you act in a respectful and tactful manner. Sadly, you hide your true abilities and accomplishments, and your uniqueness. As many times as I've shown this picture in my presentations, people actually miss seeing the difference between a cat and two raccoons! We don't necessarily hear the difference, either.

The point? People are less likely to talk with you when they are unable to distinguish a difference between you and the many others competing for their attention. Too often we keep talking because we misinterpret the other person's glazed-over look—if we even notice it at all—and instead see that look as interest in what we have to say. They become uncomfortable and will avoid you for the rest of the event.

People work with people they feel comfortable with. Unfortunately, many don't handle their networking or decision-making processes in a professional or equitable manner. It's up to you to make them comfortable while you share how you can help them be more successful. If you look and sound like everyone else, most potential business contacts won't talk with you and decision-makers won't do business with you. If you're trying to be like everyone else, they will simply shut out everything you say and think, "I've heard it all before." Or, it reminds them of a bad experience they had with someone who sounded just like you!

Whenever you hear yourself starting to sound like everyone else, stop it! Think of the cat and the raccoons. The picture is a friendly reminder that too often we like to hide out. It feels safer. However, hiding out won't pay the bills or earn you money or any well-deserved recognition. Nor will it win you a contract, award, or promotion. (*If you're looking for a job, get your copy of* It's Time to Brag! Career Edition.)

How do you show you're a winner? How do you wow others subtly but clearly while sharing your accomplishments?

Keep reading. Completing the exercises in *It's Time to Brag! Business Edition* will help you produce amazing results.

2

The Key Ingredient

On the next two pages, you will find two similar bios describing Jeannette Seibly, the author of this book. Read each one. Select the one you like best. Then ask yourself if you know the key difference between them.

INTRODUCTION #1: About the Author

Jeannette Seibly is an internationally recognized business advisor and executive coach who has worked with entrepreneurs, executives, and business owners. She has helped lots of people work smarter, enjoy financial freedom, and realize their dreams NOW. She has an uncanny ability to help her clients identify roadblocks and focus on their goals to quickly produce unprecedented results. Each client has unique challenges, and Jeannette's gift is helping each one create success in his or her own unique way. She has guided the creation of millionaires and helped companies achieve million-dollar results.

Jeannette has a B.S. in personnel administration and an M.A. in communications from Michigan State University.

She received business awards from ExperiencePros, Inc., NAWBO-Detroit, Profiles International, and DTC-CBW.

INTRODUCTION #2: About the Author

Jeannette Seibly has been an internationally recognized business advisor and executive coach for over 24 years. She has helped thousands of entrepreneurs, executives, and business owners work smarter, enjoy financial freedom, and realize their dreams NOW. Jeannette has an uncanny ability to help her clients identify roadblocks and focus quickly to produce unprecedented results. Each client has unique challenges, and Jeannette's gift is helping each one create success in his or her own unique way. Along the way, she guided the creation of three millionaires and helped over 25 companies produce million-dollar results.

Jeannette has conducted over 20 "Get Your Brag On" workshops. The workshops use the same approach she is shares in her book *It's Time to Brag!*, and in many cases the results were immediate. For example, four women increased their sales, one by $20,000 in one and a half months.

As an author, Jeannette has written four books, Hiring Amazing Employees, which sold more than 300 copies, *It's Time to Brag!, Hire Amazing Employees, Second Edition*, and *It's Time to Brag! Career Edition*. She has published over 340 articles on current management, entrepreneurial, and leadership challenges in 10 business publications, including the *Denver Business Journal* and *General Motors Leadership* publications.

Jeannette has a B.S. in personnel administration and an M.A. in communications from Michigan State University.

She has received four business awards, from ExperiencePros, Inc., NAWBO-Detroit, Profiles International, and DTC-CBW.

Which one did you like best? Which sounded more professional? Did one convey credibility faster than the other one? Which one pulled you into the conversation sooner?

Most people will say #2.

What is the key difference? Many have a difficult time distinguishing it. They'll say, "Sounds more specific." "It's more interesting." "It's more descriptive." In fact, everything is similar except for one key ingredient!

What is it?

The second bio contained numbers, metrics, and results!

It bragged!

Share Your Accomplishments

If we sound like everyone else, nobody will listen.
They've already tuned us out!

**But if we get too creative or different,
nobody understands!**
They won't take the time to find out!

Why are people not interested?
*They don't readily understand how
you can help them.*

The challenge is sharing the difference you provide.
*Share your accomplishments in a
business-savvy manner!*

When you present your results in a businesslike manner, it lets people know that you're a winner. People like to work with winners.

Relying on rhetoric obtained from websites, self-help books, sales or marketing workshops, etc. will not differentiate you from others with the same or a similar background, experience, and education. Showcasing your credentials in a business-savvy manner is important to ensure people are interested in talking with you further.

21

Remember, salespeople, consultants, business owners, executives, and entrepreneurs often believe their company is unique. If you get too creative as a way of distinguishing yourself, nobody understands you. If they don't readily understand or you're unable to talk in basic business terms, they may question your business acumen and infer a lack of knowledge or integrity on your part.

A business associate complained about not building enough credibility in her presentations. As a result, her audience ratings were lower than she intended, and she didn't develop any business leads from these speeches. At first, she resisted my coaching to do the "brag work" required to create the wow factor in her presentations; she didn't see how it would work. You can imagine my pleasant surprise when I attended an event where she was the keynote speaker and listened to the master of ceremonies introduce her. Before she said one word, she was oozing with credibility. Clearly she had decided to follow my coaching and had done the work. She had learned how to brag! It was amazing to see the audience immediately engage with her.

The exercises in the upcoming chapters will address the following questions:

- What sets you apart?
- What do your past or current clients respect you for?
- What are the positive and profound differences you've made for your bosses, coworkers, clients, and in personal and professional activities?

As stated earlier, trying to be a raccoon when you're a cat will not help you succeed!

The following is a paraphrased testimonial from a former client who is a serial entrepreneur. He started two businesses and failed because he was unable to differentiate effectively. Investors simply were not interested! After doing the exercises contained in this book, he sold his third and fourth businesses successfully. He's now working on number five.

> "I have always been impressed by people who are good at telling others what they accomplished in their career ... these people seemed amazing to me.
>
> "When I wrote down and explained what I was good at ... looked at my own accomplishments ... I started to look pretty amazing myself."
>
> – HJ

As a business owner, entrepreneur, consultant, sales or marketing rep, or someone looking to win industry recognition, you can accomplish the same results when you learn how to brag!

Many times we're unconscious of what we do, how well we do it, and the difference it makes for our employers, clients, communities, or others. We simply focus on getting the task done. We simply repeat the rhetoric we heard at a recent event. We simply tell people what we did for our past clients—not as accomplishments, but simply as things we did because we were told or expected to do them.

In the past when I introduced myself, if asked what I do, I would say, "I am a coach." Too often that would be the end of any conversation. Everyone knows lots of coaches. Nothing new. Nothing inviting. Nothing distinguishing.

However, now I say, "I'm a business advisor with over 24 years of experience, and along the way I guided the creation of three millionaires." I have their attention! It provides a differentiation. That statement invites them to continue the conversation. If they are interested in learning more, they will ask questions to start a dialogue. If not, I move on and talk with someone who is interested. Remember, spending time talking with someone who is not interested in what you do is not time well spent.

Some of you may think I'm talking about refining your elevator pitch. I'm not. It's more than that. Although you still need a one-liner, a.k.a. an objective to get their attention, if you force it without doing the work contained in *It's Time to Brag! Business Edition*, that objective will sound stilted and some of your distinguishing accomplishments will be overlooked. Your inner confidence will be missing too!

When you've completed the assignments contained in *It's Time to Brag! Business Edition* you'll also have a supporting paragraph ready to share with others. It provides credibility and tells about your successes. It elicits interest and makes others want to learn more. It increases the possibility others will want to work with you.

It gets you selected!

It gets you referred to great opportunities!

It naturally builds your confidence. And confidence has a natural tendency to shine!

This process creates a huge breakthrough. It allows you to truly see what you've accomplished. It is the first step in learning how to brag in a businesslike manner.

Remember, luck is in your preparation. Are you prepared?

Let's get started!

Keep Writing!

The key is to keep writing.
Don't stop after writing down a couple of things.
Keep writing!
When you think you're done, keep writing!
When you can't think of the answers, keep writing.
Trust the process—the breakthroughs will come.

In the next four chapters, there are five steps and exercises to move your thinking toward what you have accomplished. Don't make it harder than it is. Simply keep writing, even when you think you're finished.

Initially, you may believe the exercises are too simple. Don't be fooled by their simplicity! Many people have been, and consequently they neglected to do their work. Some were confronted by writing down their responses, others by focusing on their achievements. Although these sound like simple things to do, it's hard to write things down when it's about you. I've had people simply toss the exercises aside, never to work on them again. I've had people cry! I've had people stop, then pick up the pen again and write some more. Eventually, they had their breakthrough.

It's all in the writing. It's getting your brain to realize that you've accomplished more by writing it all down. This process takes your accomplishments out of your unconscious and forces you to think through your results. And each of you has had many, regardless of your age! This process allows you to become conscious of them. It helps you to recognize yourself as a successful business professional.

> *A business owner was struggling and needed help getting additional work from current clients and attracting new ones. After she worked on her brag statements, she shared them with her existing clients. They were so impressed by the work she had done to save them time and money, they readily referred her to new clients. (Remember, clients don't know all that you do for them—unless you tell them using your brag statements.)*

It's all in doing the work! Don't jump ahead of the instructions. Write down everything you think of. Ignore your mental monologue about the worthiness of the exercise, or your own worthiness. No one else will see this work unless, of course, you show them!

You have a multitude of unconscious reasons why you can't brag. It's an attitude you've developed over your entire life, and that attitude is why it's difficult for you to share your great results. Writing them down and getting them out of your head is the first step! These five simple exercises will help provide a structure to get you writing! When you are conscious of your successes, there is a natural difference in how you communicate with others. Your inner confidence shines. It attracts others, and they want to work with you.

Again, it cannot be forced. Shortcuts rarely have any lasting effects.

KTAs
(Knowledge, Talents, Achievements)

Step One:
Knowledge: What do you know?

The chart on the following page contains ideas to get you started. They are not inclusive. Use your own ideas or business groupings that have meaning for you. The breakthrough will only be as good as the writing you do. If you are unable to write, have someone else scribe for you. Or use transcription software that writes down what you are saying. Regardless of your age or life experiences, you've accomplished many things in your life. Simply write them all down! (Note: I realize many of you, particularly the Millennials, may want to type. It's OK; however, if possible, take the time to write out your responses. It engages the brain in a different way, helping you connect with what you are putting down on paper and have already accomplished in your career and life!)

Knowledge	Talents	Achievements
Software		
Engineering		
Human Resources		
Parenting		
Grandparenting		
Accounting		
Financial Reporting		
Perennial Gardening		
Cake Decorating		

Again, the above are simply examples to get you started.

Step Two:
Talent: Use a verb to describe your knowledge.

You can write down more than one talent to describe your knowledge. Keep them simple. The following are ideas to get you started. They are not inclusive. The breakthrough will only be as good as the writing you do. Regardless of your age or life experiences, you've accomplished many things in your life. Simply write them down!

Knowledge	Talents	Achievements
Software	Load programs	
Engineering	Calibrate variances	
Human Resources	Conduct interviews Administer benefit programs Communicate compensation changes	
Parenting	Coach Little League	
Fundraising	Sell chocolate bars for 4-H Wash cars for Boy Scouts	

Again, the above are simply examples to get you started.

Step Three:
Achievements: Use two numbers to show your results.

Achievements are where the rubber meets the road. We use two numbers to show the results we have achieved that made a positive difference. Simply talking about a task isn't inspiring to others. Achievements are why people hire you, why companies consider you a top performer. Too often business websites or people's resumes will say, "Troubleshot software issues. Handled day-to-day challenges. Sold cars. Handled administrative work for president." These don't tell us anything unique. There is no differentiation. They're examples of simply being a cat attempting to look like a raccoon!

We have conditioned our brains not to think in terms of numeric results. Numeric results require getting into the details of what we've accomplished. Becoming aware of what we've accomplished allows us to see the positive impact we've made.

Doing this level of work allows you to be more proficient when communicating your accomplishments, even though you will not be communicating all the details! When people communicate unconsciously, they are often glib, gloss over important points, and speak in a manner others don't understand. After completing these exercises, you will naturally be communicating at a more conscious level, sharing work and life experiences in a way others can relate to. It develops interest with the intention of having meaningful conversations. This is how relationships are created. It helps you get the sales contract, keep current clients, win contract bids or nominations, get promoted, or secure great work assignments!

You can write down more than one achievement to describe each talent. The following are ideas to get you started. They are *not* inclusive. The breakthrough will only be as good as the writing you do. Regardless of your age or life experiences, you've accomplished many things in your life. Simply write them down! Don't let your conversation about a poor math ability get in the way!

Knowledge	Talents	Achievements
Software	Load programs	Set up a network system for a $2MM company in three business days. Troubleshot with five clients when $150,000 software package failed to produce the results promised. Worked with three testers and developers to find the problem and resolved it within three days.
Engineering	Calibrate variances	Changed a process that saved the company $3.5MM over three years.
Human Resources	Conduct interviews	Conducted 20 interviews of systems engineers in two days. Hired five of them. All stayed with the company for three years.
	Administer benefit programs	Handled the implementation of two benefit programs for 360 employees. Terminated one pension plan to recoup overfunding of $1.3MM without any loss of benefits to the retirees.

(continued...)

Knowledge	Talents	Achievements
	Communicate compensation changes	Worked with a unionized group of 40 employees to communicate the new hourly wage, from $10/hour to $9.50/hour. This was completed without a strike and provided employees the opportunity to see that with monthly bonuses they could earn $11/hour.
Parenting	Coach Little League	Coached 15 12-year-olds to win the city league by competing against five different teams.
Fundraising	Sell chocolate bars for 4-H	Top seller of 100 candy bars for 4-H, providing the 4-H chapter $500 to spend on a trip to Washington, D.C.
	Wash cars for Boy Scouts	Participated in car wash to raise $5,000 to benefit 30 underprivileged children.

Again, the above are simply examples to get you started.

Keep writing! Many of you will not readily know your numbers. That's not a problem. Simply write down your thoughts. After you are done writing, conduct research with former coworkers or bosses, clients (don't forget past ones—it's a great way to reconnect), business associates, trade association contacts, and service professionals (CPAs, attorneys, consultants, etc.). Although most people will not investigate your numbers, you want to be as truthful as possible. If you are caught in a lie, it could easily hurt your ability to attract new opportunities or win recognition from your employer or an outside organization.

Be responsible for sharing your own numbers (a.k.a. results) along with the results and metrics of the company. People are buying your expertise to solve an issue or create a new opportunity. They need to know that you understand their concerns and have been through the same or similar experiences with successful results. This requires taking the time to listen and be present when they are sharing their issues. Use your metrics to share what you've helped others resolve in similar situations— it makes them feel comfortable that you can help them too.

As one participant said after struggling with numbers, "We all have numbers to describe our successes. It's simply becoming present to the difference we made and the results we accomplished."

The key? Stay out of mental monologues telling you this is too hard, you don't like working with numbers, or you don't believe you should have to do the work. Writing this information down will show you what you've accomplished thus far in your life. You've got years of false conditioning telling you it's not OK to brag or it's poor business manners to share your successes and achievements. Now is the time to blast through those walls, which have hindered your career, business recognition, and professional and industry credibility.

The fact that you are aware of your numbers (a.k.a. results) and are able to communicate them appropriately will definitely provide you with the advantage. Doing so will set you apart from the pack and help you differentiate yourself from everyone else attempting to do the same thing. It's like being the cat with a satisfied grin that he is a cat instead of pretending to be a raccoon.

Let me offer you some tips on how to think about your numbers. Remember, numbers can be expressed in percentages, actuals, and approximations (i.e., realistic guesstimates). Not everything is quantifiable; for example, it is difficult to measure the happiness of employees even though that may interest some people. But what you can measure is impressive: Most prospective clients and business associates will be far more interested in how many projects or consulting engagements you achieved on time and within budget. What was the budget? How long did it take to complete the project while working with and through others? What setbacks arose? How did you handle them? Did you have any turnover? Those are things that can be measured.

You may be confronted with this part of the exercise. Keep writing! I had one woman cry through the whole exercise, but she persisted. Within two weeks, she was re-employed after being unemployed for almost 18 months.

6

I AM...

---

*"Effectively communicate who you are and
the value you can provide."*
—Jeannette Seibly

Step Four:
I AM ...

Don't work on this until you've completed at least several pages of the KTAs (Knowledge, Talents, and Achievements).

In 15 words or less, describe who you are. Keep it simple and smart.

Start with the phrase, "**I am** ... "

Don't be too creative. People won't understand you or be able to readily connect with you.

As a rule of thumb, ask yourself if a 12-year-old could easily understand what you just said. If you MUST explain in order to be understood, it's not simple enough. Simple and smart brag statements create interest in you! Furthermore, if you have to explain, many people will assume you are being defensive—another reason people stop listening!

For example, I could say, "I am a coach who helps others get out of their own way." There are no numbers. But that may not be enough to generate interest in how I can help someone since it is so generic. However, if I say, "I am a business advisor who has guided the creation of three millionaires" I've created interest with struggling business owners. Or, if I say, "I'm a management consultant who helped one company reduce turnover from 125 percent to 25 percent," I have the attention of the business owner who is experiencing expensive turnover issues.

Stay away from clichés such as "I help people feel great!" or "I help companies become successful."

Don't hide the fact of what you do. If you're a salesperson seeking a promotion, you might say, "I am a sales professional and surpass my quota by 25 percent each quarter."

If you are a consultant who conducts customer service training, you could say, "I am a customer service rep who achieves 100 percent customer satisfaction." (I helped a young man who had been waiting tables win a job offer to be a customer service rep with this one!)

It helps people to readily identify with your unique qualities. This specific information, based upon what you have been successful in accomplishing with your current and past clients (and previous employers), will be of interest to your prospective client. (Note: Remember to maintain confidentiality, even if you believe they won't tell. If you tell them, they will have concerns about you telling others about them.)

Unless someone asks you a question, providing additional information after you've made your initial statement is like talking to the wall! They will not be listening! Wait until a question is asked and answer it directly with additional results.

Plan to fine-tune this all-important "I am …" statement. You may need to test it out on several people. Work with a business coach or a marketing or PR friend to help you.

Some of you will be frustrated; this information doesn't necessarily come out the first time you write it down. Or the second time. Or the third. Keep in mind that in most cases our brains have been trained to hide out and play small. Or, if we are uncomfortable talking straight, we've trained our brains to spin the facts or be highly creative. Although this may help satisfy our egos, it won't help us attract positive attention! Being genuine builds relationships.

Prospective clients must be able to readily and easily identify with how we can help them. Make sure you're using simple business words like "business advisor" or "executive coach" or "sales representative for a software engineering company" or "virtual assistant for executives" or "estate attorney" or "business owner" or "CPA." It helps others to easily understand us much faster. Stay away from cute or faddish jargon.

In addition to attracting new clients, straight talk can also produce promotions or new opportunities. It requires completing the brag exercises. Many sales reps, unconsciously or due to lack of hands-on experience, misrepresent their companies' products and services. Imagine how frustrated you would be if you started a conversation with something like "I'm looking for a financial consultant," and only after further conversation did you learn that the consultant (or their company) you were talking about didn't have the required financial experience or technology, or was trying to sell you investments that you didn't have an interest in. Learn your trade and understand the details of what you are selling and how the process works.

Talk to others how you want them to talk with you: Talk straight!

My Background Includes...

Step Five:
"My background includes ... "

This is where you bring it all together. Write one to two paragraphs about your background that describe and support your "**I am ...**" statement. Customize them for the audience. USE the NUMBERS!!!

Keep it short and to the point. Most people, including decision-makers, have short attention spans. If you're unable to grab their attention quickly, you will probably not receive the contracts or nominations you wanted, or an introduction to the right person within a targeted company.

For example, sharing one paragraph at a networking meeting will work when you are asked follow-up questions. Keep in mind that the purpose of a networking meeting isn't to sell. It's simply to create the interest to talk further.

When sending an email, writing a well-worded paragraph or two will tell others about your success and generate further interest. This more in-depth information may also induce them to introduce you to others who need your products and/or services.

Customize your background statement for your audience and use those numbers. It's amazing to me that we spend time clarifying results with numbers and then don't use them. You may wish to review my two bios in Chapter 2. In the first one I didn't use numbers, but in the second I did. See the difference? The second one bragged!

In a sales presentation, tailor your introductory paragraphs to your listener's needs. Keep it to one or two minutes. I remember one time when a person talked for 15 minutes during a sales introduction when asked the infamous question "Tell us about yourself and your company." We were all so bored with him that the outcome was determined before the sales presentation even started: NO!

In a request for proposal (RFP) or request for quote (RFQ), be sure to address the requirements up front. Again, use your numbers to demonstrate your achievements! Remember, many contract bids are awarded to companies that follow the outline they provide while also providing the wow! factor. They brag and are unafraid to share their successes in a way that makes the reader want to know more!

You may wish to hire a business coach, PR person, or sales/marketing person to help you write or edit. Do not allow them to replace the numbers. They may have not learned how to brag yet! It's commonplace that people feel uncomfortable using numbers.

Or, you could have a raving fan of your talents (for example a coworker, client, or boss) write it up for you, and then you could edit it. Resist the urge to dumb it down!

Don't forget to post these introductions on your social media pages. I've had many people tell me about how impressive my introductions are. This builds immediate credibility as a precursor to having voice-to-voice conversations with them. During the conversation, I share additional achievements that meet their interests.

The point? Take the time to write and fine-tune. Remember, your statement will need to be modified depending upon the company, industry, or profession of the person you are talking with. Take time to network with others to find out what key qualities the business you're interested in requires that are not listed on their website, PR posts, and in other product/service information. For example, if you are a consultant making a presentation to a group of small business owners about practical tips for hiring the right salesperson, it is not the same as speaking to a group of sales managers wanting to learn about motivational techniques.

Tailor your introduction accordingly. Don't forget: It's critical to build credibility in order for people to listen to your message. It makes all the difference in how they will listen to you—openly or with skepticism!

8

Practice, Practice, Practice

Like anything, mastery takes practice. Don't beat yourself up if you stumble or take the easy road by not using your numbers. Simply review and practice in front of the mirror. Keep doing your "mirror work" until the person looking back at you in the mirror gets it. If this was easy to do, I wouldn't have spent time writing a book about it.

> *I met a young professional wishing to be a realtor. She had the education and licenses. However, when she talked with people, she looked at her feet! She purchased* It's Time to Brag! *and completed the five exercises. The next time I saw her, she made eye contact, shook my hand confidently, and clearly articulated her successes in helping others find their dream homes. She had learned how to brag, and her new confidence radiated! So did her sales—she became a nationally recognized producer.*

You may get frustrated. You may be confronted. You may wish to be the cat trying to look like the raccoons. However, eventually you'll get hungry enough to want the breakthrough.

If it's too confronting, take small steps. Write down only one KTA each day. Share it with only one person per day.

You may have insights about accomplishments while you are driving to an appointment or lying in bed at night. Write them down! This flood of additional information may help you in your next networking meeting or on your next sales call or conversation with a current or future client. It can even help you with your boss! (No, they don't know all the results you've achieved for the company.)

The goal is to have people better understand who you are and identify with what you can provide for them. This understanding builds credibility faster. It will set the tone for your success.

During any type of presentation, you should plan to use your KTAs to help answer your prospective client's questions. Or, you can include them in your nomination for an industry award. A little bit of repetition, such as using the same set of numbers or examples, can help if you need to restate a particular point.

When writing sales copy, since consumers only skim it, be sure your first paragraph summarizes the company's achievements along with your numbers. You want to entice people to read further. If you're creating a website or brochure as an entrepreneur or small business owner, use your numbers and showcase your personal achievements. I think you get the idea!

You can also use the brag method to build your department, team, or business unit's sense of team loyalty. What have you achieved as a group? What are your unique qualities or areas of expertise? Voicing those accomplishments is also a great reminder of all the successful results you've had. Don't forget to share them with a client who has shown signs of straying to your competition (see Chapter 12: Create Immediate Credibility*).*

This process works! When you share your brag statements, be responsible for your tone of voice, ego, and attitude. Coming across as a braggart, regardless of whether you're a professional woman or man, will not help you. Coming across apologetically or mumbling will not work either. Simply share your successes in a straightforward manner. Ensure your attitude is positive and helpful. Keep it simple! Humility goes a long way.

Stay away from sharing any details regarding how you achieved the numbers until you get to that point in your presentation or are asked the question during a networking meeting. Then, stay away from mind-numbing details of each minute step—remember, you want them to hire you to do the work, not to train them how to do it themselves.

The goal is for business associates and prospective customers to appreciate your expertise and to hear how you helped other companies fix an issue or pursue an opportunity. You want them to understand how you can do the same for them or their clients, or for other companies they know based upon their needs. This level of conversation is normally required before being offered an introduction for a networking meeting. People want to work with winners! Winners know how to share their achievements in a professional manner that works.

Your ability to communicate your successes using numbers will forever alter the way you think and speak, and the way people relate to you. You should see results quickly.

Have fun sharing.

Enjoy bragging!

Remember, you've earned it!

Networking Works

What is networking? Many people think of networking as simply meeting others and listening to them pitch their products and services. They couldn't be further from the truth.

Savvy networkers know it's more than that.

Networking is *talking* with others to:

- Investigate new possibilities
- Become aware of new types of opportunities
- Explore new opportunities such as:
  - new technologies
  - new companies
  - new products
  - new occupations
  - new human relations/diversity concerns
  - environmental changes
  - ethical considerations
  - new business awareness required due to global competition

The challenge is that 90 percent of the world's information is in people heads! Unlocking what you need to know requires having conversations beyond 140 characters. Again, put down the phone and meet with others face to face.

Changes in business are occurring at cyber speed, and it's important to stay current and focused. Don't forget that new possibilities are being created daily. Find a niche for your skills and interests since you can't be everything to everyone. Then, learn everything you can, read trade journals, and subscribe to social media venues. Really showcase your expertise and stay focused. However, be careful about using slang or terminology in areas that are not your expertise. I've seen business professionals lose credibility quickly by misusing phrases or slang.

In order to network effectively you need to:

- Educate yourself about new opportunities
- Tap into 90 percent of the world's information, which is in people's heads
- Explore opportunities and conduct due diligence
- Contact others for information regarding best practices and policies, critical issues, best technology to use, possible solutions, etc.
- Create new opportunities for yourself by staying current on upcoming challenges and possible solutions
- Evaluate options and be prepared to negotiate knowledgably
- Make better decisions about future opportunities as they relate to your company and industry
- Make transitioning easier when you have insider information and are vying for different types of contracts in new industries

What are the added benefits of networking?

- Develops lifelong contacts so you can have great career success now and in the future
- Keeps you up to date on industry and professional changes
- Allows you to achieve your personal and professional goals faster
- Helps you resolve issues more quickly and effectively
- Provides you with information on unpublished leads and career opportunities
- Connects you with others engaged in new ventures

Why do we make networking difficult?

We are unclear about the difference between networking and selling.

An important distinction to keep in mind:
You cannot network and sell at the same time.

What's the difference between marketing and sales?
Marketing is:

- Researching issues and solutions
- Collecting information necessary to sell
- Finding new opportunities
- Educating yourself and others

Sales is:

- Presenting (i.e., sharing on-point solutions to clients' key issues and challenges)

- Conducting due diligence (i.e., knowing your potential customers' ability to pay, talking with the right decisions-makers, uncovering hidden issues)
- Closing the deal (i.e., negotiating the terms of the deal and signing the contract)

Fine-tune your clarity:
- You cannot sell and market at the same time.
- You can't sell if you don't understand the company's needs (i.e., do your market research).
- Companies buy for their own reasons, not yours.

To win a sale, we need to know the unpublished information. The purpose of networking is to tap into the 90 percent of information that is not published. Potential clients do not normally share a lot of insider information. They expect you to already know about the industry and its professional challenges and opportunities. Again, one of the values of developing relationships is to be able to connect when you need to pick their brains.

How to Do It

To keep your power and confidence, it's important that you come prepared to a networking meeting! Doing so increases your opportunity to trade information and learn about the person you are meeting with, his or her company, the profession, and the industry. Understanding and preparation on your part also prevents the person you're talking to from making a snap judgment on whether or not they would buy from you.

Important Note: Do not to take or leave behind a brochure at a networking meeting or expect the potential client to check out your website to answer their questions. Brochures, websites, and other materials are intended to support your conversations, presentations, and proposals. They don't replace the need for conversation. Failure to understand this important point will limit future opportunities with the person you're talking to and with his or her company. DO TAKE your business cards and offer them to the people you meet. Then, follow up within 24 hours by emailing a short note to say "It's pleasure to meet you." Stay away from announcing your meetings on social media venues—it can leave the other person feeling uncomfortable working or talking with you.

Keys to Conducting Effective Networking Meetings:

- You are establishing contacts that are valuable sources of information.
- You are seeking information regarding issues and potential solutions.
- You are building a network base for future business.
- You are building your lists of social media contacts.

How Do You Get Started?

Networking can be daunting if you forget the basic tenants of how to share, how to listen, and common courtesies (e.g., saying please and thank you).

Make It Easy:

- ✓ Start conversations with:
  - former bosses
  - current and previous coworkers, vendors, and suppliers
  - past and current clients
  - trade association contacts
  - professional and personal acquaintances
  - social network contacts
- ✓ Remember, geography is not important.
- ✓ Check out social media sites and websites to supplement conversations with others.
- ✓ Remember, face-to-face meetings, or using FaceTime, Skype, or other conferencing venues, are key!

How to Initiate a Meeting:

- ✓ Send an introduction email. Or, better yet, pick up the phone and call. You can also send a letter requesting a meeting. Sometimes people will prefer texts or other messaging venues.
- ✓ If you are using email or text, keep it short—a couple of paragraphs is optimal. In the Subject line, include "Referred by … " or "Requesting a Meeting."
- ✓ If you're making a phone call, use a written script that you have practiced.
- ✓ If you're writing a letter, keep it to one page. Be sure to proofread it! (Well-written letters can actually work to initially engage high-level people since they are bombarded with so many people wanting their time and attention.)

- ✓ NEVER include a brochure or other type of attachment. Prospects will simply glance at it and say no, if it is even opened.
- ✓ Never just stop by a company to set up a meeting, even if you already know the person!
- ✓ Meetings should be no longer than 20 minutes.

How to Schedule the Meeting:

Here is language you can use to get people to open your email, text, letter, or answer your phone call. Keep in mind that it is your responsibility to follow up with a call, text, or email to schedule the meeting. If you contact the person via phone, it's up to you to request the meeting. Here are some helpful tips for crafting an effective message:

- ✓ Use the "I am …" statement you have developed.
- ✓ Include that you are "seeking to learn more about your company, product, or service …"
- ✓ Include the name of the person who referred you and share in 10 words or less what you discussed.
- ✓ Mention that he or she "said you would be a valuable source of information on this topic."
- ✓ Say, "I would welcome the opportunity to meet with you."
- ✓ Provide two to three sentences outlining your background. Be sure they are on point with the topic to be discussed.
- ✓ Close with "I will contact you on X to set up a convenient time to talk." (Be sure you follow up!)

The Actual Face-to-Face Meeting: First Impressions Matter!

- ✓ Arrive 5–10 minutes early. (If using Skype, FaceTime, or another conferencing technology, be sure it's working before the meeting!)
- ✓ Dress professionally. Be clean and neat. (Yes, this is true even when you're not physically meeting face to face.)
- ✓ Don't chew gum.
- ✓ To help connect with the person faster, wear a tie/scarf, suit, or shirt/blouse that matches your eye color.
- ✓ Always be nice to the receptionist, assistant, or the server at the restaurant or coffee shop where you meet.
- ✓ Shake hands and provide a business card.
- ✓ Do not leave your brochure, web link, or DVD!

The Actual Meeting: Getting Off on the Right Foot

- ✓ Introduce yourself by clearly stating your first and last names.
- ✓ Extend your hand for a handshake.
- ✓ Be sure you're looking them in the eyes.
- ✓ Make a statement about the person who introduced you by stating that person's full name and add that he or she "said that you would be a valuable source of information."

The Actual Meeting: The Meeting!

This is where most people lose control of the networking meeting and the other person turns it into a yes or no meeting.

✓ Thank them for meeting with you.

✓ Restate the full name of the person who referred you and add that "they said you would be a valuable source of information." (Yes, this is an intentional repeat.)

✓ Reiterate the time frame for the meeting: "As I shared when setting up this meeting, I plan on taking about 20 minutes and have specific questions to ask."

✓ Remind them you are here to simply learn more about their industry, profession, and/or company.

✓ Set the tone. Share your "I am …" and "My background includes … " statements.

Ask questions designed to answer the following. Use a conversational tone; this is not an interrogation!

✓ "Tell me about you." What is the person's background, years in their profession, years in the industry, etc.?

✓ "What would you consider to be the biggest issue?" What are three problems or needs of the industry, profession, or company?

✓ "What do you believe is/are the possible solutions?" What are three possible solutions, qualifications required to address them, company's interest in resolutions?

The Actual Meeting: Summary

✓ Although your research prior to your meeting should have prepared you for key issues, it's important to recap the top three issues discussed and your background in those areas in how you've addressed them—don't forget to include your numbers! Remember, the key issues may be different than anticipated.

✓ Ask, "How can I help you?"

The Actual Meeting: Asking for Referrals

Ask who they would recommend that you speak with next:

✓ "Of the people you are professionally or personally associated with, who would you recommend I talk with further about _____?"

✓ "Could you suggest other people you are professionally associated with to talk to about _____?"

Note: Be aware of simply being given a name and contact information. Request the person send an introduction email or make a social media connection to both of you. This will increase the likelihood that the referred person will respond to you.

The Actual Meeting: End of Meeting

✓ Thank them for their time.
✓ Shake hands and exit.
✓ Do **NOT** leave brochures or other written materials.
✓ **Do** leave a business card.

After the Meeting

✓ Send the person a thank you email, text, letter, or card within 24 hours.

✓ Include any information that you promised to provide.

✓ Send a thank you to the person who referred you. They may have additional contacts for you to talk with and will be glad that you followed up and followed through on their suggestion.

Review – Part I (Immediately Afterwards) – Write down or note on your electronic device the following (do not rely on your memory):

✓ Who did I talk with: title, background, company?

✓ What did I learn about the department, company, industry, profession, issues, company, or industry jargon?

✓ What are the problems and issues for the company, department, industry, or profession?

✓ What are possible solutions?

✓ How does this align with my company's purpose, interests, and expertise?

✓ Who can I refer this person to if my company doesn't handle those interests or doesn't have that expertise? (Send an introduction email or social media invitation to set up a conversation after you've received permission from both parties.)

Review – Part II (After 24 Hours) – Time to think through the following questions. I find it helps to write down my thoughts.

✓ What changes do I need to make in my presentation?

✓ Am I asking the right questions?

✓ Am I getting the type of information I need?

✓ Am I being referred to the right people?

✓ If not, whom do I talk with?

✓ Do I need to update my "I am ... " and "My background includes ..." statements?

Do

✓ Be prepared with an agenda

✓ Treat this as an important meeting

✓ Ask and expect referrals

✓ Actively listen

✓ Be coachable if asking for advice on a professional or personal matter

✓ Practice, practice, practice *before* each meeting

✓ Determine a weekly goal of meetings, and follow through

✓ Update your social media sites (e.g., LinkedIn, Facebook, Twitter, etc.) weekly with positive comments

Don't

✓ Fall into the "interview you" trap

✓ Leave behind a brochure or other unrequested written information

✓ Get defensive

✓ Get into political or religious discussions

✓ Vent your frustrations

✓ Post information about your meeting with the person on social media

✓ Post inappropriate comments on your social media sites
✓ Conduct meetings with high-level decision-makers without having conducted at least three other networking meetings previously with people who can tell you about the person and his or her company, business practices, and internal challenges

Whether you are starting out in a new job or profession, or have advanced in your career, making the time to network is critical. It's important to develop and keep important relationships. You never know when things may change and you may need to reach out for help—or, others may need to tap you on the shoulder for help. To meet the right people and keep your network viable, make the time to meet and expand the types of people you engage with, as well as the types of events you attend.

The key is to keep your network alive and well. Following up and following through are two of the most important steps. Networking works when you stay in touch with others and are available if they need anything. If you only contact your network when you need something, people will stop helping you!

Effective networking means you can work smarter, not harder. Often, people who effectively conduct networking meetings enjoy it! Beware of the trap of confusing lots of activity with achieving your intended result, such as closing your next sale, winning an award, and/or getting to the right decision-maker.

Questions to Ask Yourself:

- ✓ Are you getting the types of introductions that fit your goals?
- ✓ Are you getting closer to meeting the right decision-maker(s)?
- ✓ Are you getting closer to finding new opportunities? If not, what do you need to transform? (Note: Consider that it could be your attitude or belief about yourself and others if you're not getting the type of information or contacts you need.)
- ✓ Talk with your coach, mentor, or a friend for insight. We all have blind spots. It takes someone else's insight to help us see more clearly.

10

Conduct Your
Preliminary Research

Too often in our haste and because of poor planning, we fail to stop and consider the purpose of our meetings. Always take the time to conduct preliminary research. Be open to the fact that those you talk to may have a different goal or view of what they need. Be prepared to refer them to more appropriate vendors when opportunities present themselves during network meetings, with their permission. The biggest mistake many make when networking is promising they can deliver a product or service for a particular purpose that is not a match for what the company needs.

Before the Meeting

Read their company website. Google the name of the company and its products and services. Google the name of the person you are meeting. Contact your network for information that is not published (remember, 90 percent of the world's information is in other people's heads!). Check out both the company's and your contact's social media information (e.g., LinkedIn, Facebook, Google+, Twitter, etc.). Subscribe to their feeds to see what you can learn about their products and services.

During the Network Meeting

Most salespeople, business owners, and consultants make huge mistakes by assuming they know how a company operates. Always have good business questions ready, regardless of whether you've worked for this company, boss, or team members, or if you have done business with the company in the past. Perspectives and business practices change with new bosses and employees, and with time. Ask questions, probe, and openly listen to the responses without judgment.

Write your questions down and take the list with you. Some ideas to get you started:

- ✓ What type of challenges has the company experienced? (Be sure you've done your online and network investigation.)
- ✓ Are they aware of what started the issue?
- ✓ What do they believe are the solutions?
- ✓ What results did they achieve when they implemented these solutions?
- ✓ What do they believe is the next logical step?
- ✓ What will get in their way of taking it?

Keep in mind that confidentiality is important.

The biggest challenge for most people after networking meetings is following up and following through. Outline with the other person what you will provide him or her and by when you will do so. Then, call to ensure he or she received the information and determine what the next step is. Developing positive relationships is important. Many base their future interactions on the person's ability to do what they say they will do. It also will make a difference when it comes time to close the sale.

Close the Sale

We've been talking about networking and marketing yourself and your company in a positive way to establish credibility upfront. These efforts make a significant difference in your ability to compete for the sale. Now it's time to use your brag material to help you close the sale, win the award, or receive the contract bid.

When writing out a draft of your accomplishments for a sales presentation, an award nomination, or a contract bid, use your KTAs as the outline. From there, include the other information required by the RFP, RFQ, industry, or company in their submission instructions. When answering these questions, use your brag statements. For example, if the question is "How many times have you xx?" a potential answer might be "In the past xx years, we have handled xx projects resulting in $xx in sales."

Company and industry awards may be internally driven and subjective. When they are, be sure to let your boss know verbally and in writing of your achievements after each project. He or she can often provide you additional information or contacts to help you better understand the process and what information will make the difference in vying for the award. For internal recognition, she or he can provide any insights into office politics and additional resources that may be required to support you and your team to achieve the goal. Many times, awards are based upon how well a submission is written—be sure to have it professionally reviewed before sending it in.

Remember, include any networking information (aka insider information) appropriately to stay on point with their concerns, along with your metrics and accomplishments.

If you don't win the sale or the award, call the decision-maker to get clarity about what was missing in your submission or presentation and include this information in the future.

12

Create Immediate Credibility

When preparing the introduction for your sales presentation or speech, outline your brag statements. Then include your "I am …" and "My background includes … " statements to share in your introduction and periodically throughout your talk. Don't forget to include your numbers! Remember to keep the message short and on point, usually one to three paragraphs. Long-winded introductions rarely make a good impression, build credibility, or keep most people's attention.

LinkedIn and Social Media Venues

Use this process to create brag statements for your products or services. Share them on your social media venues, in particular LinkedIn. Check out mine at *www.linkedin.com/in/jeannetteseibly.*

Attracting New Clients

Being referred to a decision-maker by a networking source can make it an easier sale. First, they will review your online presence before they talk with you. Be sure they are wowed by what they read by using your brag statements and the information provided to them by the person introducing you. If you are offering the referral, I find introducing both parties in an email to be a great practice. Then, let them connect with each other. Another method is to invite them both to coffee or lunch and provide an introduction at that time (include a link for their background information using their website and/or LinkedIn profile). If you are the recipient of the referral, when you receive these types of emails respond quickly and don't attempt to sell at this time by providing marketing slogans.

When setting up meetings, be flexible and meet where it is most convenient for the potential client. During the meeting, narrow in on the top reason you can help them, and stay focused. Trying to provide too much too soon with too many possibilities usually ends with the potential client postponing their decision to work with you, then, after a period of time, deciding to not move forward with you. Remember to keep it simple and smart when providing quotes and proposals.

Straying Client

If you have a straying client, prepare a list of all the activities and results you've provided to the company or your contact. Be sure to use your KTAs as an outline. If you are a sales representative, consultant, or the business owner, share them when renewing contracts or looking to increase your sales through upselling or cross-selling. Most clients are unaware of what you have done for them, the money you've saved them, and the results achieved. By using this method, several of my clients have held on to large clients who were being wooed by the competition.

Group Brags

Don't forget another great idea (mentioned in Chapter 8) of using the brag method within your department, team, or business unit. What have you achieved as a group? What are your unique qualities or areas of expertise? Exploring these questions is a great way to build team loyalty and share the wealth of knowledge and information your team can provide. It's also a great reminder of all the successful results you've had with a client who may be considering a move to your competition.

13

Invaluable Career Wisdom

It's an attitude:
Your attitude is an asset or a liability.
It's your choice.

Commitment is the key to success in any career, for any business group, or in any entrepreneurial venture. Too often we say that we're committed to something; however, when we don't follow through, attend meetings on time, or engage others effectively, people question our commitment—even when we have the best of excuses! A lack of commitment, for whatever reason, makes people question the quality of products and services that you can provide and whether you are someone they want to do business with.

Your professional and personal attitudes and behaviors are also important. You may have the commitment but you lack a can-do attitude and struggle to attract the right prospects and close sales. A positive attitude influences your sales, industry, or professional recognition and career options, now and in the future. It's why some people get introductions to others' networks or are invited to present their products and services, even though they have fewer qualifications than you.

Brag statements, networking, and building credibility are important skills if you want to have a satisfying career and develop professionally over your lifetime. They are great reflections of a positive and confident attitude, *when you share them.*

For many people who are self-employed, independent contractors, or in sales, it can be hard to stay positive and do the required work daily. In Chapter 14, you'll find some exercises to keep your mindset positive. They can easily be done between meetings; at the end of the day, week, or month; or on an as-needed basis. In addition, on the next couple of pages you'll find some tips to maintain your image as a powerful business professional.

Luck Is Preparation!

As a successful business professional, consultant, or executive, it's always important to be prepared and develop the technical, financial, sales, management, and project skills required, even if you need to pay for the courses, workshops, or books yourself. Some opportunities may only appear once! After a while, they will stop if you are not ready and willing to do the work required. Stop blaming your employer (or boss or yourself) if you have not acquired the skills you need. These excuses will not get the job done. Take responsibility! Companies want to work with winners to solve their challenges or concerns.

Additional Items for You to Consider:

- Keep financial debt to a minimum (preferably, have none at all). Too often opportunities come along that people cannot take advantage of because they can't afford it.

Keep your credit scores high and keep your credit report clean. Some businesses run financial checks before doing business with you.

- Take time to learn new skills (software, Internet, music, gardening, public speaking, writing, negotiating, etc.). Share about them on your social media sites.

- Develop yourself professionally and personally by learning new things about how to elicit the best in yourself and others, and what gets in your way when working with others or achieving goals. This requires more than attending a life-changing event, buying into a new concept, or watching a master performance and then trying to adopt it as your own. Take away one or two insights from these experiences and put together a structure for fulfilling the revelations they gave you. Work with your coach or your industry mentor to ensure you use these insights appropriately.

- Remember, self-confidence is important as a way to get others to share their insider information with you. Use brag statements to communicate your achievements!

- Don't stretch the truth during meetings: Answer the prospective client's questions appropriately and honestly using your brag statements. Don't respond with what you think they want to hear. In addition, learn to ask questions for clarification. Otherwise, you will often be wrong. Major career derailment happens if you make a sale and your customers feel they were scammed. Having a client say,

"There is nothing worse than working with a liar!" can be demoralizing.

- Take time to reassess your life goals periodically. Life does change, and so do your goals, personal and professional needs, and aspirations.

- Know your strengths and weaknesses, since truly understanding yourself gives you a competitive edge. Use a qualified assessment to help you clarify them and learn who you are, not who you want to be. Go to *http://SeibCo.com/contact* to learn more about what a qualified assessment is and why using one is important.

- Don't be a lone ranger. Ask for help. Be willing to accept help graciously.

- Make it a habit to send thank you notes!

- Hire an experienced coach and find a mentor in your industry. Issues that people would like to discuss with a coach include becoming more effective, developing business and professional savvy, developing confidence, having someone to bounce ideas off of, and handling problems that arise. With an industry mentor, it's important to keep up with changes. Most successful business professionals and executives have their own coaches and mentors! Focus on their experience and successes when deciding to hire them.

- Get involved in and attend trade or professional association meetings. Be sure that your efforts are in alignment with the type of client you can help. For example, attending a mergers and acquisitions meeting may be interesting; however, if you and/or your company don't provide those types of services, it's taking your time away from meeting the right people in groups where your expertise is needed.

- Life has a way of getting our attention, particularly when we don't want to listen! When you experience challenges with bosses, employees, clients, or if you are bored or unwilling to do your job, hire a coach or therapist! Find out why now, before it's too late to get help with your career choices.

- Respect all people you meet, and their opinions and feelings. You can achieve this by listening more than talking, maintaining confidentiality, returning all phone calls within 24 to 48 hours, keeping your commitments and following up quickly, dressing for success, arriving at least five minutes early for each meeting, posting appropriate messages on your social media sites, and having a professionally scripted voicemail message.

- Remember, companies select vendors and suppliers for their own reasons, not yours. You cannot sell unless you understand their needs. Do not burn bridges by telling current or future clients they were wrong to offer the contract to someone else. Stay in touch. If it was the wrong vendor, they may be calling you soon.

- Always, always, always go to a meeting prepared. It doesn't take that much time to Google the company's name and its products and services, and read the information. The biggest error is when salespeople or business consultants believe they understand an organization's culture, issues, and possible solutions, even though they never worked for that company.

- Stop trying to be a mind reader. Too often we take the tiniest bits of information and believe we know what the person is trying to say by adding our own meaning to it. You will often be wrong, and therefore you'll lose out on professional opportunities, obtaining important information, and being offered leads or other needed support to be successful.

The bottom line is this: Stop waiting for the perfect time or the opportunities will diminish. Learn how to brag! Showcase your confidence and credentials by effectively using your brag statements when networking, presenting, and writing. Achieving industry or professional recognition isn't that hard when you've learned how to brag in a business-savvy manner.

Keep your copy of *It's Time to Brag! Business Edition* and update your brag statements periodically to keep you prepared for your next amazing opportunity.

14

Mindfulness Keeps You Moving Forward

"It takes courage to do what you need to do for yourself.

It takes more courage to do it in a manner that leaves others inspired by your efforts."
—*Jeannette Seibly*

What is mindfulness? It refers to conscious awareness or presence. Improving this will help you stay in business, win contracts, and have amazing conversations that lead to great business opportunities. It requires you to put down the phone and engage in face-to-face conversations (including conversations on FaceTime and Skype).

Being an entrepreneur, solo-preneur, salesperson, consultant, or business owner will have its ups and downs. Staying positive and courageous when things are not going well can be a challenge, and too often people will check out mentally or emotionally. This is when mindfulness is critical to working through the issues, having the breakthroughs, and building on the outcomes.

Get into the habit of talking to yourself and about yourself in a positive way. Your positive mental monologue will improve how you feel about yourself and others. Conversely, if you allow negative feelings to fester, your mental monologue will jump in to create stories about yourself and others and hurt your efforts. Unfortunately, as human beings we can take the tiniest fragments of information, nonverbal cues, or words and misinterpret as well as personalize them. The ego takes over, and it's downhill from there. Being mindful is the best way to catch these actions or attitudes quickly and correct them even faster!

The following are simple ways to remind yourself that you are a great person and can offer great products and/or services to others. When you feel good about yourself, you will normally feel good about others. People want to work with winners.

Brag!

On a daily, weekly, and/or monthly basis, write out your "I am …." and "My background includes …" statements. Review them and post them on your mirror. Rewrite them in your journal. Share them with others. This will help reinforce your achievements, and you will exude natural confidence.

The "I Am" Alphabet

Use the alphabet to create "I choose to be …" "I am …" or "I have …" statements. Have fun and enjoy coming up with one word for each letter of the alphabet to describe yourself.

Keep in mind there are many choices!

Start with: I choose to be …. (Or, I am …. Or, I have …) and go through the alphabet.

(Example: I choose to be joyful. (Or, I am joy. Or, I have joy.)

A = Assertive

B = Brilliant

C = Competent

…

These can be done first thing in the morning or before you fall asleep at night. Also, use them while you are driving to an appointment or when you have had a challenging day. Any time is the right time.

What Good Things Happened This Morning, This Afternoon, or Today?

You can answer this question at any time during the day, before you fall asleep at night, after a meeting, or on your way to your next meeting. If you journal, this is a great question to answer in addition to listing those things you are grateful for.

Stay Fit Mentally, Physically, and Emotionally

Walk it out. Walk or run at least a mile per day or do any other type of aerobic exercise that you enjoy. Another fun way to keep your body moving is to use a pedometer. Set a target and achieve it each day.

Talk it out. Talk with a few select and trusted coworkers or a boss when confronted with a challenge. Hire a coach or business advisor, even if you need to pay for it yourself. Talk to the clergy of your religion. Or, commit to seeing a licensed and trained professional on a consistent basis until you have resolved any personal or professional challenges. Keep in contact with others via social media venues as well as face to face! Stay involved in social activities. Refrain from engaging in "ain't it awful" sessions on social media, in networking groups, or when attending workshops or seminars. Remember, what you share can come back to haunt you!

Write it out. Keep a diary or journal. It's not for the benefit of others but for voicing your opportunities and challenges in writing. Studies show that writing things down can make a huge difference. Do not send hate letters or nasty emails, texts, or other types of messages when situations do not go your way or when you are upset. It could cost you your job, client, or opportunity.

Improve Your Results … What Worked? What Didn't Work?

This one will require you to write down your responses to receive the greatest benefit.

Too often we are unaware of what is going well or specifically what needs to be fine-tuned to achieve our intended results. We create a blanket statement about the project or client being difficult, good, or great. It can ruin our day if we are solely focused on the negative or miss completing necessary details because we glossed over the work that needs to be done.

You can base this exercise on a project, customer, or sales process when things seem to be unworkable or you have become overwhelmed. Set aside 20 minutes and complete the following exercise. It's also good to complete daily, weekly, monthly, and annually and any other time period that is meaningful to you.

What Worked? Start here—too often we automatically go to the negative or the excuses. Using metrics, list all the things that are working. To get started, write down the key aspects of the job, project, or customer that has been working. For example, "XYZ customer loved the proposal since it saved them $xx."

What Did Not Work? Second, using your numbers (or metrics) list all the things that specifically are not working. For example, "Missed my goal during Q1 to increase sales by ___percent." Stay away from excuses.

Review the First Two Categories. Don't forget to include anything else that is important to you, the project, your boss, your clients, the team, etc.

What Would You Like to Be Acknowledged For? Yes, human beings hate to be acknowledged! Write down the acknowledgments you would like to receive. Use short phrases, for example, "I increased attendance to 100 percent at team meetings." It really does feels good!

Keep Writing Even after You Believe You Are Finished. Don't forget to quantify your results or activities: "Improved xxx system by decreasing time spent by xxx percent." This helps you clarify what you've achieved rather than simply stating, "I worked fewer hours on xxxx." You'll find it inspiring to see you've accomplished more than you originally thought. Then, update your KTAs for future brag statements!

Now, share this information with the "person in the mirror" if you do not have another person or small group to share it with. This process can be cathartic. It rids you of self-limiting conversations based upon excuses and "shoulds," and it's also a great team exercise for getting everyone on the same page. It can refocus you on specific actions to get you back on track while opening up conversations with others to handle missed results. It will naturally rejuvenate your personal satisfaction and professional commitment, and that of your team.

Now, it's time to get your brag on!

Share!

Enjoy your amazing results!

About the Author

Straight talk with dynamic results!

Jeannette Seibly has been an internationally recognized business advisor for over 24 years, with a total of 38 years working with entrepreneurs, executives, and business owners. She has helped hundreds of companies use job fit technology to improve retention, hire the right person for the right job and team, and create strategy for high-impact results. Her work with thousands of sales professionals, business consultants, executives, and small business owners makes a positive difference in helping them wow prospective clients and industry leaders faster. Along the way, three executives became millionaires and Jeannette helped create 25 new executives.

Jeannette has earned the right to brag. Her savvy tips and techniques will show you how to create your own bragging rights during networking meeting and sales presentations, and by winning coveted industry recognition.

How to Work with the Author

To learn more about Jeannette Seibly and her other products and services, contact her at *www.SeibCo.com/contact.*

"Straight talk with dynamic results"

Contact Jeannette for a complimentary discussion.
Jeannette provides the following services:

Business Advisor – Achieves dynamic results one on one with business owners and executives.

Management Consultant – Manages people for results, designs strategic hiring and promotion systems for profitability, and uses qualified assessments for job fit.

Facilitator – Transforms outcomes with management teams and boards of directors, and gets everyone on the same page.

Join the conversation on Facebook at
http://facebook.com/TimeToBrag
and share your successes!

Made in the USA
Middletown, DE
16 October 2016